ABIGAIL ADAMS

COURAGEOUS PATRIOT AND FIRST LADY

SPECIAL LIVES IN HISTORY THAT BECOME

Signature LIVES

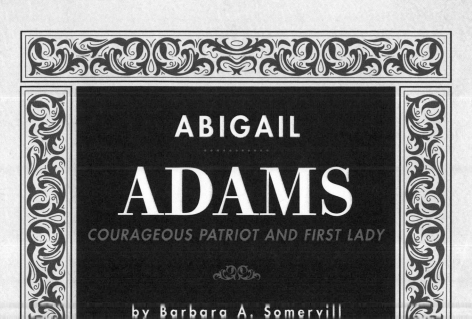

ABIGAIL
ADAMS
COURAGEOUS PATRIOT AND FIRST LADY

by Barbara A. Somervill

Content Adviser: Margaret A. Hogan,
Associate Editor, The Adams Papers,
Boston, Massachusetts

Reading Adviser: Rosemary G. Palmer, Ph.D.,
Department of Literacy, College of Education,
Boise State University

COMPASS POINT BOOKS  MINNEAPOLIS, MINNESOTA

Compass Point Books
3109 West 50th Street, #115
Minneapolis, MN 55410

Visit Compass Point Books on the Internet at *www.compasspointbooks.com*
or e-mail your request to *custserv@compasspointbooks.com*

Editor: Sue Vander Hook
Lead Designer: Jaime Martens
Photo Researcher: Svetlana Zhurkin
Page Production: Noumenon Creative
Cartographer: XNR Productions, Inc.
Educational Consultant: Diane Smolinski

Managing Editor: Catherine Neitge
Creative Director: Keith Griffin
Editorial Director: Carol Jones

Library of Congress Cataloging-in-Publication Data
Somervill, Barbara A.
    Abigail Adams / by Barbara A. Somervill.
        p. cm—(Signature lives)
    Includes bibliographical references and index.
    ISBN 0-7565-0981-5 (hardcover)
    1. Adams, Abigail, 1744-1818—Juvenile literature. 2. Presidents'
        spouses—United States—Biography—Juvenile literature. I. Title.
        II. Series.

E322.1.A38S66 2006
973.4'4'092—dc22   2005002704

REVOLUTIONARY WAR ERA

The American Revolution created heroes, and traitors, who shaped the birth of a new nation—the United States of America. "Taxation without representation" was a serious problem for the American colonies during the mid-1700s. Great Britain imposed harsh taxes and refused to give the colonists a voice in their own government. The colonists rebelled and declared their independence from Britain—the war was on.

Table of Contents

1 FOUNDING MOTHER

❧❧❦❧❧

On top of Breed's Hill in Charlestown, Massachusetts, a group of ragtag soldiers lined up behind a crude stone barrier. They were ready to fire on the most powerful nation on earth. It was June 17, 1775, and the powerful nation was England. The ill-equipped soldiers were American colonists, called rebels, who were willing to fight and die for the freedom they wanted so much.

The rebels planned to take their position on Bunker Hill, but in the dark of night on June 16, they quietly moved to nearby Breed's Hill. Nearly surrounded by water on a peninsula overlooking Boston Harbor, the militia had only a narrow neck of land for retreat. The 1,200 rebels were far outnumbered by the powerful, red-uniformed British

Colonists take their positions behind a makeshift wall as the British march up Breed's Hill in Charlestown, Massachusetts.

army of more than 7,000. The rebels had too few weapons, too little ammunition, and minimal training. But their bravery and resolve made up for what they lacked in skill and equipment.

Bostonians watched the Battle of Bunker Hill from their rooftops on June 17, 1775.

A command passed through the rebel lines: "Don't shoot until you see the whites of their

eyes!" The British started up the hill. The rebels took aim and fired their muskets. The British returned fire. Bullets flew, and hundreds of soldiers lay dead or wounded on the hillside. The British retreated and regrouped.

For hours, the thunder of battle rolled over the land. People in neighboring Boston heard the gunfire and saw the billows of smoke rising in the sky. They clambered to hilltops to see what was happening. They positioned themselves on top of buildings and church steeples to watch the battle rage. On nearby Penn's Hill stood 30-year-old Abigail Adams and her 7-year old son, John Quincy Adams. They watched in amazement as their friends and neighbors were wounded and killed.

A second assault of British soldiers charged Breed's Hill, and smoke once more filled the air. Rebel troops again sent the redcoats on the run, but the British would not be stopped. They regrouped and charged the hill again. This time, the colonists were defenseless. Their gunpowder was gone, and using rocks and rifle butts for weapons was useless. The British swarmed over the barricade and overtook them. About 440 rebel soldiers died that day, and 30 were captured.

The British won the Battle of Bunker Hill, as it came to be called, but they paid a high price—1,054 casualties. It seemed unusual, but the Americans actually celebrated. They had successfully held off the highly trained British army until the ammunition ran out. Now they knew the British could be stopped, and they were determined to keep on fighting for independence.

The day after the battle, Abigail Adams put her quill pen to a piece of paper and described the fight in a letter to her husband John, who was in Philadelphia, Pennsylvania:

> *Sunday June 18 1775*
>
> *Dearest Friend,*
> *The Day; perhaps the decisive Day is come on which the fate of America depends. My bursting Heart must find vent at my pen. I have just heard that our dear Friend Dr. Warren is no more but fell gloriously fighting for his Country ... great is our Loss. ... God is a refuge for us,—Charlestown is laid in ashes. ... How [many ha]ve fallen we know not—the constant roar of the cannon is so [distress]sing that we can not Eat, Drink, or Sleep.*

Little did Abigail realize the many personal sacrifices that lay ahead for her and her family. She had already been apart from her beloved husband, who was involved in political discussions. Even as the Battle of Bunker Hill was seething, John Adams was meeting with the Continental Congress to discuss

American grievances against the British government. It was there that John received his wife's letter and read the vivid details of the skirmish.

For the next several years, Abigail wrote to her husband almost daily, keeping him informed about what was going on in the Revolutionary War. She longed to be with him but knew how important his work was. He was helping to shape the budding new

Painter John Trumbull served in the Continental Army and witnessed the Battle of Bunker Hill. His 1786 painting shows the death of American General Joseph Warren.

United States of America.

Life was busy for Abigail while John was gone. She managed the family farm, coped with food shortages, and raised and educated their children by herself. She was teacher, nurse, cook, seamstress, and laundress. She hired farmworkers, wove cloth, sewed clothes, and made soap. She also concocted herbal

A painting of John Adams by John Singleton Copley, America's first great portrait artist

medicines from plants in her garden and fended off British soldiers who were invading Boston homes. If it got really dangerous, John advised her, "Fly to the woods with our children."

Abigail Adams didn't hesitate to use her letters to influence the laws of the new nation. At a time when English law allowed men to own their wives, she bravely encouraged her husband to "remember the ladies" of this infant country, so their lives would be better than they had been in the past.

John Adams' brief response—"I cannot but laugh"—sent Abigail back to her pen and paper with a letter to her friend Mercy Otis Warren: "I ventured to speak a word in behalf of our sex, who are rather hardly dealt with by the laws of England."

It also bothered Abigail that girls seldom received a formal education. She brought this up with her husband. "If we mean to have heroes, statesmen and philosophers, we should have learned women," she wrote. This time, her husband agreed:

> *Your sentiments on the importance of education in women are exactly agreeable to my own.*

Whenever she had the opportunity, Abigail Adams quietly wrote down her strong opinions. She corresponded regularly with Warren and once wrote to Catharine Macaulay, a British writer who thought the American colonies should not be ruled by England.

Abigail Adams described the Battle of Bunker Hill in this letter to her husband John.

These women used pen and paper to express their opinions. Abigail Adams had an impact on Founding Fathers like Thomas Jefferson, and she entertained George and Martha Washington at her dinner table. Her influence continued when she entered political life as the wife of the first vice president of the United States and then as first lady. She educated and nurtured the sixth president of the United States—her son, John Quincy Adams.

In spite of Abigail Adams' directions to her husband to burn all their letters, John Adams preserved them, leaving an important account of the Revolutionary War era. The letters also give a clear picture of who Abigail Adams really was—courageous patriot, founding mother, and significant first lady of the young United States. ஒ

Abigail Adams (1744-1818), American patriot and wife of John Adams, the second president of the United States

Chapter

2 COLONIAL GIRL

ରେଜ୍ଞ

Thirty years before the Revolutionary War broke out, life in Massachusetts was interesting and busy. In 1744, the year Abigail Smith was born, cobblers went from house to house measuring feet and making shoes for colonial families. Coopers made barrels for storing flour, dried corn, and salt pork. At the chandler's shop, fishermen bought rope, canvas, and tar for their ships. In Boston Harbor, traders unloaded barrels of molasses from ships, to be used for making rum. Farmers tended corn and beans in nearby fields and grazed cows and sheep in the center of town.

On Sundays in Weymouth, Massachusetts, the shoemakers, sailors, blacksmiths, coopers, farmers, and their families headed to the Congregational

Colonists take part in a singing procession during a New England religious revival in 1740.

Church. The children fidgeted on the hard wooden pews, and the Reverend William Smith preached about sin and salvation. Sunday dinner, prayers, and Bible reading filled the rest of the day.

November 11, 1744, was a special day for Smith and his wife, Elizabeth Quincy Smith. That was the day they

A Puritan minister preaches from a pulpit in a Boston church.

welcomed their second child—Abigail—into the world. Their other daughter, Mary, was 3 years old when her sister Abigail was born. Two more children, William and Betsy, would later complete the Smith family.

Massachusetts Bay Colony was home to several generations of Smiths. Abigail's father came from a long line of ministers. Abigail's mother was a member of the Quincy family, one of the prominent families in Massachusetts. The Smiths and the Quincys were highly respected by this community of strong religious colonists.

The Smith home was comfortable and easygoing. Her father was kind and generous. Her mother often took her daughters Mary, Abigail, and Betsy to visit the sick, the elderly, and the poor. Abigail learned that those who have more money must help those in need.

Abigail was a bright young girl who liked to learn. But formal education was important only for boys at that time. Boys went to school and studied

In the 1700s, some colonists worked at jobs that are rare today. Cobblers made shoes by hand. Blacksmiths made horseshoes, pots, pans, and metal tools. Coopers turned wood into leakproof barrels, and tanners worked animal skins into leather for shoes, clothes, bags, and belts. Millers ground grain into flour, while chandlers sold supplies for ships. Sometimes people's last names were taken from their occupations. Their names were Chandler, Smith, Cooper, or Miller.

reading, writing, Latin, and arithmetic. They learned how to hunt and fish, earn a living in a trade, or run a farm. For girls, it was considered more important to learn how to be wives and run a household. Some girls went to the one-room schoolhouse, but most were taught at home in a dame school, where the teacher was their mother or grandmother. There they learned to read, write, and do math—but only enough to run a home. Abigail and her sisters never received any formal education, and Abigail thought this was unfair. She wanted to be as well-educated as her brother and father.

Instead, Abigail was trained to be a wife, mother, and homemaker, which was not an easy job. There were no vacuum cleaners, electricity, supermarkets, or refrigerators. Heat came from wood-burning stoves and fireplaces. Laundry water was heated over the fire, and dirty clothes were swirled in a bath of harsh lye soap. Then, women squeezed out the water by hand, hung out the wash to dry, and ironed each piece of clothing with a metal iron heated on the stove. Because there were no bathrooms, bathing was usually a quick wash, often with cold water carried in from outside. As for a toilet, the trip to the outhouse was a brisk walk, especially during snowy winter months.

The Smiths produced their own food by gardening, hunting, fishing, or butchering farm animals.

A young colonial girl peels apples for her mother.

Spring for Abigail and her family meant hoeing, planting, weeding, and tending the garden. Summer brought drying beans, cutting corn, and preparing fruits. Potatoes, carrots, onions, parsnips, and turnips were harvested and stored in cool cellars. In autumn, hogs and beef cattle were slaughtered. Men hunted deer, wild turkey, and other game. Meat and fish were cut and either packed in salt and spices or smoked. When all the work was done, the family hopefully had enough food for the winter.

Abigail learned how to bake bread, make soap, dip candles, and mix herbal medicines. When someone was sick, women served as nurses and used the herbal remedies handed down from their mothers. Weaving fabric and hand-stitching cloth into shirts, pants, and dresses occupied what little time colonial

A typical colonial kitchen during the Revolutionary War era.

girls and women had left.

Abigail's father liked to indulge his children by letting them go through books in his large library. They read history, famous sermons, and poetry by Shakespeare and John Milton. They learned about politics, religion, philosophy, and drama. They knew about the world beyond Weymouth.

Abigail spent as much time as she could reading, studying, and learning. But this was most unbecoming for a young colonial girl. An educated woman risked being shunned by potential husbands. Most men did not want a woman who could think on her own. They wanted good housewives and strong mothers for their children. When 23-year-old John Adams first met the Smith girls, he thought they were intelligent, cold, distant, and snobbish. But two years later, John and Abigail met again. This time, his feelings were different for 17-year-old Abigail.

John began writing to Abigail, and he stopped in Weymouth whenever he could. As a young lawyer trying to build a practice, he often traveled to different courts throughout Massachusetts. He welcomed the trips that took him near the Smith parsonage on a Sunday afternoon, where he could get to know Abigail better. His own home was a house in Braintree, Massachusetts, that he had recently inherited from his father. He could look out his window at 10 acres (4 hectares) of apple trees, open

This saltbox cottage was the birthplace of John Adams. It is located in Braintree (now Quincy), Massachusetts.

fields, and forest. The square-shaped cottage, called a saltbox, provided an adequate roof over his head.

In his little cottage, he often wrote letters to Abigail. He now addressed her as "Miss Adorable" and ordered her to give him "as many Kisses, and as many Hours of your Company ... as he shall please to Demand." Abigail often expressed her deep feelings for John in her letters:

> *And there is a tye more binding than Humanity, and stronger than Friendship, which makes us anxious for the happiness and welfare of those to whom it binds us. It makes their Misfortunes, Sorrows, and afflictions, our own.*

They playfully gave each other names from ancient history or classical mythology. John was Lysander, the Greek general; Abigail was sometimes Diana, the goddess of purity, and at other times she was Portia, the sensible Roman woman and Shakespeare's fearless heroine. Abigail wrote a letter to John on August 11, 1763:

> *Judge you then for your Diana has she not this day had sufficient cause for pain and anxiety of mind? ... The health and happiness of Seneca she says was not dearer to his Paulina, than that of Lysander to his Diana. ... Accept this hasty Scrawl warm from the Heart of Your Sincere Diana.*

Their relationship grew stronger over the next two years. The love and unique intellectual companionship they shared would last through war, hardship, and separation. ✒

3 STARTING A FAMILY

Chapter

❧❧❧

By colonial standards, Abigail Smith and John Adams had a long courtship. John worried about how he would support a wife and family with a struggling law practice. But he knew Abigail was the only one for him.

Even though she was still a teenager, Abigail had a mature outlook on life. She was not pretty by society's standards. Most people probably would have called her "interesting." Her face was oval with a sharp, pointy chin, and she had a long, thin nose and narrow lips. Her most striking feature must have been her eyes, which were described as brilliant, piercing dark brown. John, on the other hand, had a round, fleshy face, a lumpy nose, a stout body, and stubby legs. His blue eyes sank beneath thick, heavy eyelids. As different as they were in appearance,

Portrait of Abigail Smith Adams as a young woman

they were alike intellectually. John admired Abigail's brains and encouraged her desire to learn.

John and Abigail also had very different backgrounds. Abigail Smith's family was the cream of colonial society, but John Adams came from a family of farmers and cobblers. He had recently received a degree from Harvard College and was working as a lawyer. Some thought John and Abigail were an unlikely combination, but the couple married on October 25, 1764. The Reverend Smith presided at his daughter's ceremony in the Weymouth meetinghouse. Abigail was just shy of her 20th birthday, and John would turn 29 in five days.

The newlyweds moved into John Adams' little saltbox house in Braintree. John set up his law office and library in a downstairs room. Abigail took over the kitchen, where she cooked, sewed, and read books. The small parlor made a nice place to greet guests.

John and Abigail Adams had plenty of land to grow corn, potatoes, pumpkins, squash, onions, and herbs. They had half a dozen cows, a small flock of sheep, and chickens. Abigail milked the cows, collected eggs from the chickens, and tended the garden with help from Judah, the hired servant. Their apple orchard provided fruit for pies and cider, and the wooded area supplied enough firewood for the kitchen stove and fireplaces.

John Adams was often away from home, traveling to several courts throughout the colony. He would try

Abigail Adams, like many colonial women, milked dairy cows every day to provide milk for her family.

cases in Boston one day, then Salem, Plymouth, or Worcester the next. Legal work provided him with a natural connection to politics. Colonists had been uneasy about their relationship with Great Britain for 10 years, and John was concerned. Great Britain and France were also in conflict, having fought the French and Indian War on North American soil from 1754 to 1763. Great Britain won the war, but it had cost them a lot of money. The British government decided the colonists should pay for the war, since it had been fought on their land.

To force colonists to pay for the war, Great Britain imposed taxes on many imported and exported items. The Molasses Act of 1733 had affected colonial businessmen who had to pay fees on the molasses they imported. The Stamp Act of 1765 affected all the colonists. Any printed item—newspapers, bills,

> *Molasses is syrup extracted from sugarcane. In the 1760s, African slaves were forced to produce molasses on the islands of the Caribbean. Molasses was shipped in barrels to the American colonies to be turned into rum. The colonists then sold rum to Great Britain, and the money was used to buy more slaves in Africa who could produce more molasses from sugarcane.*

pamphlets, deeds, wills, business contracts, licenses, almanacs, and even playing cards—had to be stamped to show that a tax had been paid.

The Stamp Act affected John and Abigail Adams. John had to pay for every will, deed, or contract that he wrote in his legal practice. He even had to pay taxes on bills he sent to his clients. The taxes also affected their home. They had to pay taxes on their newspapers, pamphlets, and bills. Every piece of paper with printing on it had to bear a stamp. The colonists were not happy about these taxes.

Even so, the British weren't done angering the colonists. They passed yet another law—the Quartering Act—that required the colonies to house and feed the British soldiers in their communities. Soldiers could live in barracks, taverns, or private homes, but the colonists had to pay for it. This also outraged the colonists. They demanded that if they were to be taxed, they should have a representative voice in the British Parliament. Their cry rang out, "No taxation without representation!" A group of colonists called the Sons of Liberty soon rose up in

New York City to protest the unfair taxes and laws. Their message quickly spread to other colonies.

Colonial merchants responded to the unfair laws by banding together to boycott British goods like wool, calico, sugar, coffee, tea, and wine. They also refused to buy English china, crystal, silverware, furniture, soaps, perfumes, silks, and linens. John Adams joined in the protests. Abigail Adams quickly adjusted to the changes created by the protests. Supporting the boycott meant not buying any products England shipped to the colonies. Even goods made in Europe had to go through British ports, which further limited what the colonists could buy.

Citizens of Boston read news of the Stamp Act in August 1765,

During a debate over the Stamp Act of 1765, Isaac Barré referred to Americans opposing the tax as the "Sons of Liberty." Groups formed and gave themselves that name. The first group formed in New York City in the fall of 1765. Not all their tactics were peaceful. In 1766, the Sons of Liberty interrupted the opening performance at a new theater in New York City shouting, "Liberty!" and forced the audience into the street. The group pulled down the building and set it on fire.

On July 14, 1765, in the midst of the political conflicts, Abigail Adams gave birth to their first child. They named her Abigail but called her Nabby. The delighted mother wrote that they were "blessed with a charming Girl whose pretty Smiles already delight my Heart, who is the Dear Image of her still Dearer Pappa."

During the next year, Abigail raised Nabby, and John became more involved with protests and politics. He won a seat on the Braintree town council, his first elected position and the start of a new career. He and his fellow colonists continued to protest the Stamp Act so strongly that Parliament finally repealed it in March 1766. Throughout Boston, "Bells rung. Cannons were fired. Drums beaten." John took part in the celebrations, but Abigail celebrated quietly at home since she was ill that day.

The British government had been defeated—for a time. But the defeat of the Stamp Act did not stop Parliament from imposing more taxes. Almost in an act of defiance, the British passed the Declaratory Act,

which said Parliament had the right to tax its citizens, and it had every intention of doing so. Soon, Britain imposed the Townshend Revenue Acts, requiring colonists to pay taxes on paper, tea, glass, paints, and lead. Although many Bostonians remained loyal to Great Britain and King George III, they didn't agree with the endless taxation. Again, the Adamses and other colonists boycotted British goods.

Angry citizens of Boston rioted in the streets in 1765 in protest against the Stamp Act.

Colonists devised other ways to get the goods they needed. They even smuggled supplies into their cities and towns. In May 1767, Britain reacted to these smuggling practices. Weighed down with cannons, British warships moved into Boston Harbor to catch the smugglers. One of the first people the British accused of smuggling was wealthy shipping baron John Hancock. He was brought to court, but his lawyer, John Adams himself, managed to get the British to drop the charges.

In the middle of the boycott, the crisis over taxation, and the Hancock trial, Abigail Adams gave birth to their second child—John Quincy—on July 11, 1767. A delighted John Adams wrote about his children to his good friend and brother-in-law Richard Cranch:

> *Johnny must go to Colledge, and Nabby must have fine Cloaths ... and there must be dancing Schools and Boarding Schools, and all that.*

A year and a half later, the couple welcomed another daughter into their family. Sadly, Susanna was a very sickly baby and lived only 13 months. Abigail often worried about her children's health. Far too many families lost at least one child to diseases like smallpox, chicken pox, diphtheria, measles, mumps, rubella, or the flu. The list of diseases that took the colonists' children seemed endless.

As the family grew, so did John's law practice. Every day, he traveled eight miles (12.8 kilometers) on horseback or in a horse-drawn wagon between Brainteee and Boston. Brutal weather, rain, and rut-

The Old State House (center) in downtown Boston was the heart of Massachusetts political life.

ted dirt roads frequently made the trip very unpleasant, so he decided to move his family to Boston.

There, the Adamses rented a home on Brattle Street, just two blocks from the Old State House where the government and the Massachusetts courts met. The house was ideal, except for the noise made by British soldiers training on their street. British troops were all over Boston, patrolling the streets and making citizens angry. Abigail didn't want soldiers living in her neighborhood or practicing their drills on her street. Neither did the other residents of Boston. Tension filled the air. ✎

4 MASSACRE IN BOSTON

❧❧❧

British occupation of Boston made the city seem like an army camp. Tempers flared as citizens tried to avoid the red-uniformed street patrols. On March 5, 1770, a lone British soldier stood watch on a Boston street. Rowdy young colonial men challenged him, shouting names like "lobsterback" and "redcoat" and daring him to shoot them.

A crowd gathered, and the soldier sent for support. British Captain Thomas Preston and some of his troops joined the frustrated soldier. The mob hurled snowballs and stones at them, while more insults erupted. Suddenly, a shot rang out—and then more, in a volley of gunfire that left 11 colonists wounded on the street. Five of them— Samuel Gray, Crispus Attucks, James Caldwell, Samuel Maverick, and Patrick Carr—died of their wounds.

A line of British soldiers fires on a crowd of unarmed colonists in an attack that came to be known as the Boston Massacre.

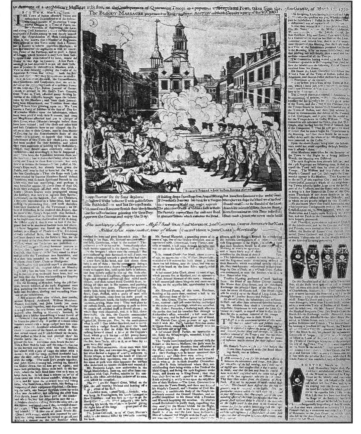

Bostonians were angry. Mobs swarmed the
streets, set on violence and revenge. Colonists
quickly arrested British soldiers and their captain.
John Adams hurried home to Abigail and the children. Abigail, pregnant with their fourth child, was
anxious and shaken by this horrible event that came
to be called the Boston Massacre.

As a lawyer and public servant for a British-ruled
colony, John Adams was obligated to represent eight

British soldiers involved in the Boston Massacre. The trial began in October 1770, and John stayed in Boston most of the time. Abigail was left alone in Braintree with their children, Nabby, John Quincy, and now 5-month-old Charles, born on May 29, 1770.

John Adams finally won a not-guilty verdict for six of his defendants. Two others were found guilty of manslaughter and were branded with a hot iron and released. The not-guilty verdicts proved to be highly unpopular among the colonists. Many people had hoped all the soldiers would be hanged. Again, tension was high in the streets of Boston.

On September 15, 1772, the Adamses welcomed another son, Thomas Boylston, into the world. Now, with a daughter and three sons to raise and a husband who traveled almost continuously, Abigail often felt burdened with responsibility. The family sometimes lived in Boston to be near John's work and sometimes stayed at the farm in Braintree. Nearly all the duties of raising the family and tending to the farm fell on Abigail's shoulders.

In May 1773, the British Parliament imposed another new tax—the Tea Act. Tea was the most pop-

> *Branding was a common punishment in colonial times. A convicted criminal had a letter burned onto his thumb with a hot branding iron. The letter indicated the crime that had been committed—M stood for manslaughter, T for thief, and so on.*

ular drink in the colonies, among all ages. A tax on top of the cost of tea was punishing for most citizens. Abigail, along with most of the other colonists, planned a boycott and refused to buy, drink, or serve British tea.

When this tax was imposed, the Adamses had been living in Braintree. Now they went back to Boston, where John could be at the center of what was happening in law and politics. Events stirred up by the Tea Act came to a head. John wrote in his diary on December 17, 1773:

An English cartoon poked fun at a group of American women who signed an agreement not to drink tea or purchase British goods.

Last Night, 3 Cargoes of Bohea Tea were emptied into the Sea. ... This is the most magnificent Movement of All. ... To let [the tea] be landed, would be giving up the Principle of Taxation by Parliamentary Authority, against which the Continent have struggled for 10 years.

On the night of the Boston Tea Party, as it came to be called, Abigail was visiting her parents in Weymouth. She hadn't heard the whole story about the colonists who had disguised themselves as Indians and dumped British tea into Boston Harbor. She wrote to her husband:

If you have any news in Town which the papers do not communicate, pray be so good as the Write it. We have not heard one Word respecting the Tea at the Cape or elsewhere.

In May 1774, an angry British Parliament passed the Coercive Acts, which the colonists called the Intolerable Acts. The laws restricted use of the waterways and regulated the cargo on colonial ships and barges. The acts

Late at night on December 16, 1773, a group of Boston colonists dressed as Indians crept aboard British ships docked in Boston Harbor. In a protest against the unfair Tea Act, the colonists opened crates of tea and poured the leaves into the harbor. This "tea party" cost the British the equivalent of more than $1 million today.

served as a punishment and a restriction for the citizens of Boston. Britain also passed the Boston Port Act, which stopped colonists from receiving or shipping anything at Boston Harbor. A closed port meant merchants could not receive anything from across the seas or from other colonies. Boston had effectively been shut down and cut off from the world.

Other laws soon followed. The Massachusetts Provincial Council, the governing body for the Massachusetts Bay Colony, was now controlled by a British governor. Citizens could not elect their own representatives, and British officials accused of a crime were to be tried back home in England.

John Adams decided it was time to move his family out of Boston. Abigail and the children returned to their home in Braintree, where Abigail immediately started managing the farm. John continued to work from his law office in Boston. He kept Abigail informed of what was happening there. He wrote to her:

> We live, my dear soul, in an age of trial. What will be the consequence, I know not. The town of Boston, for aught I can see, must suffer martyrdom.

In September 1774, representatives from all 13 colonies met in Philadelphia to discuss the Intolerable Acts. John Adams represented Massachusetts at this meeting of the Continental Congress. Little did Abigail know that this first long separation from her husband would become the pattern of their lives for the next 10 years.

Abigail wrote letters to John almost every day while he was in Philadelphia. She told him how the British had seized the colonists' gunpowder from the arsenal at Charlestown and how worried she was:

I will not despair, but will believe that, our cause being good, we shall finally prevail. The maxim "In time of peace prepare for war" ... resounds through the country. Next Tuesday they are warned at Braintree, all above fifteen and under sixty, to attend with their arms; and to train once a fort- night [two week period] from that time.

The First and Second Continental Congresses of 1774 and 1775 met at Carpenter's Hall in Philadelphia, Pennsylvania.

For Boston-area residents, life was a struggle. Vast numbers of British redcoats marched through the towns, and all non-British ships and vessels were turned away from Boston Harbor. Supplies were scarce, and only British goods were available. Of course, Abigail Adams and other colonists supporting a boycott refused to buy British goods, so their provisions were dwindling to nothing. She wrote to her husband:

> *As for me, I will seek wool and flax, and work willingly with my hands; and indeed there is occasion for all our industry and economy.*

True to her word, Abigail did work hard. She found ways to feed her children, educate them, nurse them back to health, and tend to all their needs. Since John's law practice was put on hold while he attended the Continental Congress, their only income was what Abigail earned from the farm. They learned that every penny was important.

Even with the help of hired servants, Abigail's chores filled her days and nights. Gardens needed hoeing, planting, weeding, and harvesting. Cows needed to be milked twice a day, cream had to be churned into butter, and cheese had to be made. Wool from sheep was spun into thread and woven into cloth. Apples needed to be picked, pressed into

A colonial woman spins thread in her home to make cloth.

cider, and placed in cool cellars for the winter. Laundry piled up to be washed by hand, hung out to dry, and ironed. Nights were spent knitting, sewing, and repairing a mountain of clothing.

Through it all, Abigail Adams ached with loneliness. She wrote to her beloved husband, "My Much Loved Friend, I dare not express to you … how ardently I long for your return." But she also was determined to work as hard as she could so her husband could stay in Philadelphia and do his part for the cause of freedom. ᕉ

5 WOMAN OF THE REVOLUTION

❧✦❧

The winter of 1774-1775 was difficult for Abigail Adams at the Braintree farm. British taxes were a financial burden, and the numerous boycotts made supplies scarce. But things were even worse in Boston. Redcoats still paraded through the streets, and colonists were growing more anxious. By spring, frayed nerves erupted into squabbles on both sides.

By April 1775, Britain's General Gage had had enough. He obtained a warrant for the arrest of two of his worst enemies—John Hancock and Samuel Adams, a second cousin of John Adams. The two men fled Boston, with British soldiers close behind, and headed for Hancock's house in Lexington, Massachusetts. On the night of April 18, Paul Revere and a few other patriots hurriedly rode through Concord and Lexington to warn

Colonial minutemen, ready to fight at a minute's notice, take aim at the British at Lexington, Massachusetts, on April 19, 1775.

the citizens, including Hancock and Adams. "The British are coming!" they shouted as they rode through the streets. As dawn broke, Hancock and Adams fled Lexington, while the Massachusetts minutemen gathered on Lexington Green. The British arrived, and shots were fired. The American Revolutionary War had begun.

John Adams was still in Philadelphia, now at the second meeting of the Continental Congress. In her letters, Abigail kept her husband informed of what she knew about the war. On May 24, 1775, she wrote:

> *The report was to them, that three hundred had landed, and were upon their march up to into Town. ... Our people landed upon [the] Island, and in an instant set fire to the Hay which with the Barn was soon consumed.*

Nearly every household in the Boston area became involved in the war. Fathers and sons left home to go fight, while family members who stayed home were forced to house and feed British soldiers. There was no end to the shortages—firewood, lamp oil, candles, coffee, tea, chocolate, and more. Some Bostonians left their homes for safer places, and British soldiers quickly occupied their houses. The soldiers drank the ale, wine, and cider left behind, and burned the furniture for heat.

Even the Adamses' Boston home was occupied— by a British doctor—which greatly concerned

Abigail. She asked her relatives to check on the condition of the house, and they found the place filthy. Items had been stolen from the home or destroyed, yet the structure of the house remained in fairly good condition. Abigail wrote to her husband:

> *Soldiers comeing in for lodging, for Breakfast, for Supper, for Drink. … Sometimes refugees from Boston tired and fatigued, seek an assilum for a Day or Night, a week—you can hardly imagine how we live.*

The war affected the prices of common household items, and soon, many items were no longer affordable.

Abigail sent an urgent note to John:

> *Purchase me a bundle of pins and put them in your trunk for me. The cry for pins is so great that what I used to buy for seven shillings and sixpence are now twenty shillings, and not to be had for that.*

Finally, some good news came to Abigail and the people of Massachusetts. At the recommendation of her husband, the Second Continental Congress declared that the colonial soldiers in Boston were now officially an army. Congress appointed George Washington to be the general of the new Continental Army. John Adams said:

> *Congress have made choice of the modest and virtuous, the amiable, generous, and brave George Washington, Esquire, to be General of the American army, and that he is to repair, as soon as possible, to the camp before Boston.*

Before Washington could get to Boston, a battle had begun on Breed's Hill in Charlestown, Massachusetts. It was June 17, 1775. Abigail Adams and little John Quincy watched on top of Penn's Hill as the colonists, now the Continental Army, fought the powerful British. The colonists lost this battle, called the Battle of Bunker Hill, but now they believed they could win the war. These agitated and angry colonists had the encouragement and momentum to keep on fighting.

Two weeks later, Washington entered the city of Cambridge, Massachusetts, to take command of the Continental Army. Abigail was there when he arrived. Delighted with the general, she wrote her husband:

> *I was struck with General Washington. ... Dignity with ease ... the gentleman and soldier, look agreeably blended in him. Modesty marks every line and feature of his face.*

George Washington takes command of the Continental Army on July 3, 1775.

Unfortunately, Washington was given an army with

little experience, few weapons, and not much food. Compared to the British, they were outnumbered and outgunned—and soon to be run out of Massachusetts. At least, that was what the British hoped.

Colonists were eager to join Washington's Army. Some of the farmers on the Adamses' land in Braintree decided to join up. The cash that Abigail earned from these farmers who rented her land was cut off. The ones who stayed agreed to work for her, but they demanded a high wage. With few workers available, Abigail had no choice but to pay them what they demanded. Most men were going off to war, and there was already a shortage of food. She couldn't risk her family starving through the winter. Worried, she wrote to John in Philadelphia:

> *Grain, grain is what we want here. Meat we have enough. … We shall very soon have no coffee, nor sugar, nor pepper.*

For a while, things went well at Braintree. Ten-year-old Nabby helped in the kitchen and tended to the younger boys' needs. She sewed and mended their clothes. John Quincy (age 8), Charles (age 5), and Tom (age 3) wanted to be soldiers and join the Army. Of course, that wasn't possible, and Abigail continued to give them a solid education daily at their kitchen table.

Then, disaster struck Massachusetts. Dysentery swept through the entire colony. Old and young, strong and weak fell ill from the disease. Few were spared in the Adams household. The sickness first seized Abigail, and then other family members became ill. She wrote to John:

> *Our home is a hospital in every part; and what with my own weakness and distress of mind for my family, I have been unhappy enough.*

Young Thomas suffered badly and recovered slowly. One of the servants died after being sick for weeks. Abigail's own mother died of the disease

The kitchen in the Adams house in Braintree (now Quincy), Massachusetts.

American colonists made many of their own medicines. They used cinnamon and nutmeg to stop vomiting and reduce nausea. Cloves would kill whatever germs were causing dysentery, they thought. Rhubarb root and Indian root might ease diarrhea. These herbs could be dangerous if people took too much or got a poor quality herb.

after coming to care for Abigail when she was sick with the ailment. Medicine was scarce, and Abigail asked her husband to send herbs and spices like turkey rhubarb root, nutmegs, cloves, and cinnamon, to help them through the illness.

By early 1776, the Adams household and other colonial families had recovered from dysentery. While many were weak with illness, the fight for American independence had grown stronger.

Nearly every colonist who could read was poring over a small pamphlet titled *Common Sense*, written by Thomas Paine in February 1776. John Adams sent Abigail a copy, and she was quite moved by Paine's challenge to the colonies to form their own government separate from the British.

John Adams, Thomas Jefferson, and Benjamin Franklin were working diligently in Philadelphia to create a document that would declare the colonies' independence from England. Finally, they decided what the document should say, and Jefferson wrote what was called the Declaration of Independence.

Abigail Adams was also busy writing. With the colonies on the verge of independence and the

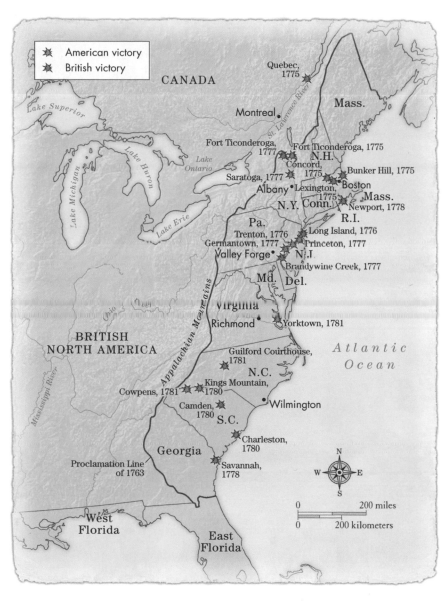

American victory
British victory

CANADA

Lake Superior

Quebec, 1775

Montreal

Mass.

N.H.

Lake Michigan

Lake Huron

Lake Ontario

St. Lawrence River

Fort Ticonderoga, 1777

Fort Ticonderoga, 1775

Concord, 1775

Saratoga, 1777

Albany

Lexington, 1775

Bunker Hill, 1775

Boston

Mass.

Lake Erie

N.Y.

Conn.

Newport, 1778

R.I.

Pa.

Trenton, 1776

Long Island, 1776

Germantown, 1777

Princeton, 1777

Valley Forge

N.J.

Brandywine Creek, 1777

Md.

Del.

Ohio River

Appalachian Mountains

Virginia

Richmond

Yorktown, 1781

BRITISH
NORTH AMERICA

Guilford Courthouse, 1781

*Atlantic
Ocean*

N.C.

Cowpens, 1781

Kings Mountain, 1780

Camden, 1780

Wilmington

S.C.

Mississippi River

Georgia

Charleston, 1780

Proclamation Line
of 1763

Savannah, 1778

N
W   E
S

0   200 miles
0   200 kilometers

West
Florida

East
Florida

Founding Fathers discussing the laws for a new nation, now was the time for her to speak up for the rights of women.

Major battles of the American Revolution were fought throughout the colonies.

Abigail Adams'
handwritten
letter to her
husband, John,
reminded him
to "Remember
the Ladies"
when the new
laws of the
nation were
formed.

She urged her husband:

*[B]y the way in the new Code of Laws
which I suppose it will be necessary for you
to make I desire you would Remember
the Ladies, and be more generous and
favourable to them than your ancestors.*

Her letter even contained a rather serious threat:

If perticuliar care and attention is not paid to the Laidies we are determined to foment [stir up] a Rebelion.

John Adams responded lightheartedly—"I cannot but laugh"—to Abigail's extraordinary request for those times. His response did not set well with Abigail. Hoping to gain support for her cause, she wrote to her friend Mercy Otis Warren, whose brother James Otis had written about the emancipation of women more than a decade earlier. Mercy did not respond to her letter, and Abigail was never sure why.

In the middle of April 1776, Abigail was again in Boston. She watched as the British army marched out of the city, forced out by Washington's Army. Washington guessed that New York City would be their next target, and he was right. In a few months, 10,000 British troops invaded New York.

With the British gone from Boston, the city began to recover, and Boston Harbor again opened for business. Goods poured in and filled the shops, although prices remained high. Abigail was worried—would the British go next to Philadelphia, where John was still meeting with the Second Continental Congress?

6 SACRIFICES FOR A NEW NATION

❧❀❧

The British did, indeed, march proudly into Philadelphia, Pennsylvania, on September 26, 1777. However, most of the residents had abandoned the city by that time, including John Adams, who had returned home to Abigail and the children. He had been gone off and on for nearly four years and had missed watching his children grow up. Nabby was almost a teenager, and John Quincy had become a young man of 10. Charles was 7, and 5-year-old Thomas was no longer a baby. John planned to reopen his law practice and not accept any political office that might be offered to him. But that was not to happen.

The Congress of the young nation called on John Adams again. Would he help arrange an alliance

John Adams and his 11-year-old son, John Quincy Adams, sailed to France on the Boston *in 1778.*

between France and the infant United States? Adams wondered how he could help, since he spoke no French and had no experience in diplomacy. In fact, he was brutally honest, tactless, and fiery tempered. Although these were not the characteristics of a diplomat, he agreed to go to France.

Adams wanted to take the whole family with him to Paris, but the voyage was much too dangerous. He compromised by just taking 11-year-old John Quincy. Now Abigail would be separated from her husband and her oldest son. She worried that the cold mid-winter voyage across the Atlantic Ocean would end in disaster. With British enemy warships all over the sea, she wondered if her husband and son would survive.

There was no way to keep things cold on the *Boston*, so Abigail helped her husband pack live animals. When they needed meat for meals, the animals could be butchered and cooked right on the ship. She gathered hogs, sheep, and chickens to send with her husband and young son. She packed barrels of dried corn, cases of rum, tea, chocolate, brown sugar, mustard, pepper, and apples. Of course, she didn't forget to put in paper, quill pens, and ink so John could write to her. She also packed books, clay pipes, tobacco, and pistols (just in case).

On February 14, 1778, father and son set sail. The six-week voyage was miserable. The ship stank of stale water, mold, and human waste. Heavy gales sent stomachs heaving, adding yet another foul odor to the air. In April, they arrived in Paris and stayed with Benjamin Franklin, who was there to ask France for help with the war.

Despite the importance of what her husband was going to do in France, Abigail Adams longed for his return. She had willingly agreed to be apart from her husband for the cause of freedom, but she constantly tired of her life alone. Managing the farm in Braintree left her struggling to make ends meet. To help out, John sent items from France—pins, handkerchiefs, ribbon, calico cloth, anything she could use or sell. She quickly made a nice profit from selling French wares in the Boston area.

Negotiations with France went well over the next 18 months, as Franklin, Adams, and others convinced the French government to help the colonies in their fight for independence. They even called on France's King Louis XVI and dined at the royal court with his queen, Marie Antoinette.

While Benjamin Franklin was in France, he lived in the small town of Passy, just outside Paris. He was very popular with the French.

Marie Antoinette, queen of France during the French Revolution, was the wife of King Louis XVI. She was later beheaded by her own subjects in 1793.

Adams was impressed with the queen:

> She was an object to sublime and beautiful for my dull pen to describe. ... She had a fine complexion indicating her perfect health, and ... not a feature of her face, nor a motion of any part of her person ... could be criticized as out of order.

Finally, in the summer of 1779, John Adams finished his work in France and came home. He and his son arrived at Boston Harbor aboard *La Sensible*. It was harvest time at the Braintree farm, and John pitched in right away to help with the chores. Abigail was delighted to have her husband and son home, and she was ready to resume a normal family life.

But it was not to be. A few months later, Congress asked John Adams to go back to France. Although the battles were still raging on American soil, Congress wanted Adams to begin negotiating peace and trade agreements with Great Britain and European and African countries. John couldn't turn down the request, and Abigail would not stop him from doing the important work of the newly formed United States. She gave her blessings to her husband, and on November 15, 1779, he boarded *La Sensible* again and set sail for France. This time, he took along two of his sons—John Quincy and Charles.

For Abigail Adams, this was the hardest and longest separation yet. Months turned into years, and soon, more than four years had passed. John repeatedly begged his wife to join him in Europe, but the farm and her ailing father kept her in Massachusetts. Early in 1784, however, Abigail had enough, and she packed her bags to go to Europe. She took along Nabby, two servants, a cow, and trunks filled with clothes, dishes, and books. Young Thomas, however,

While John Quincy Adams was in France with his father, he traveled throughout Europe and went to school in Paris and Amsterdam. At an early age, he learned to speak French and some Dutch. In 1781, at the age of 14, he traveled to Russia with Francis Dana, the U.S. representative to that country. He served as Dana's private secretary and interpreter of the French language. Adams was only 15 years old when he returned to Paris to help informally with the peace treaty that would end the American Revolution. In 1825, John Quincy Adams became the sixth president of the United States.

stayed in Massachusetts with Abigail's sister.

Abigail believed their ship, the *Active*, must have been named for the endless rolling and heaving at sea. She and Nabby both suffered from seasickness. Typical of her strong and determined will, Abigail still helped out on the ship. She taught the cook how to properly prepare food and the crew how to clean. During the four-week trip, she supervised daily cabin cleaning and proper dishwashing.

They arrived in London on July 21, 1784. Nine days later, John Quincy arrived from France to welcome them. Abigail was astonished by the changes in her son. He was now 17, tall, slim, blond, and energetic. He was good-humored and mature for his age.

A week later, John Adams also arrived in London, and Abigail was reunited with her beloved husband. The four of them traveled back to France, and for the next nine months, they lived in a rented 30-room

The home of Abigail and John Adams in Auteuil, France

house in Auteuil, France, about four miles (6.4 km) from Paris. Ben Franklin's home in Passy was nearby, and the large Bois de Boulogne park was close enough for them to enjoy. Abigail and John became good friends with Thomas Jefferson, who lived in Paris.

The home suited Abigail, but the hired servants did not. She was used to a few servants who did a great deal of work. In Paris, she had a large number of servants, each doing specific jobs, and not all that well. Abigail missed life in Massachusetts. She felt that Paris was no place for a preacher's daughter like her.

The following year, in 1785, John Adams was named the first U.S. minister, or representative, to Great Britain. That meant Abigail had to pack and move once again, this time to London. John Quincy returned to Massachusetts, where he attended

Harvard College. Abigail, John, and Nabby headed to London, where they rented a three-story house in Grosvenor Square with an attic, where the servants lived. As expensive and wasteful as she found Paris, Abigail thought London was even more so.

Although she did not like extravagant living, Abigail Adams found herself in the royal court of the king and queen of England one day in 1785. She spent nearly all day getting ready for the event. But even with her best clothes and jewelry, she didn't feel like she fit in. Abigail found King George III, Queen Charlotte Sophia, and their princess daughters quite rude. The only purpose for being there

The royal family of England: King George III and Queen Charlotte Sophia in the center, surrounded by some of their 15 children.

was to flatter and please the British royalty. Abigail still remembered all too well how the colonists had suffered during the Revolutionary War to get rid of this royal power, and she did not like pleasing them.

While in London, Nabby married William Smith, a colonel in the American legation, or embassy, in Great Britain. Abigail was happy about her daughter's marriage, but she was still not happy with London life. Prices were so high that she wrote their friend Thomas Jefferson in Paris, asking him to buy satin slippers, men's socks, fabric, pins, and everyday items for her. But what Abigail really wanted was to go home. She said:

> [R]etiring to our own little farm, feeding my poultry and improving my garden has more charms for my fancy than residing at the court.

It was three years before Abigail got to go home. John Adams was negotiating peace and trade agreements with the countries of Morocco, Portugal, and Great Britain. But finally, at Adams' request, Congress recalled him from his duties. The couple returned home to Braintree in 1788. The new country of the United States was working on its Constitution. Soon, the people would elect their first president and vice president. Abigail's dreams of a quiet life again would have to wait. ᨒ

7 RETURN TO POLITICS

Chapter

❦

The arrival of John and Abigail Adams in Boston, Massachusetts, in 1788, turned into a citywide celebration. John had done important work as U.S. minister to Great Britain, and the citizens of Massachusetts were grateful and proud. For a while, John and Abigail stayed with John Hancock in his mansion on Beacon Hill in Boston, but Abigail just wanted to go home to Braintree.

But "home" was not the former farm. While in London, John Adams had purchased a new house with 14 acres (5.6 hectares) in Braintree, and that's where they went. They named their new home Peacefield. The house was not in good condition, and it definitely needed repairs and Abigail's personal touch. She cleaned, unpacked boxes, planned

George Washington (center) is inaugurated as the first president of the United States. Vice President John Adams is on his left.

meals, and bought food. Abigail was happy to be home. She never regretted giving up appearances at the royal court for the simple gatherings in her parlor at Peacefield. She didn't miss the seven-course state dinners—she preferred the soup, main course, and corn pudding at the family table. Nor did she need dozens of servants—just a few was enough.

Her husband, on the other hand, did not know what he would do now. John Adams faced an uncertain future. His choices were to rebuild his law practice or return to political life once again.

It wasn't long before he again entered the political scene—this time on the 1789 ballot as a candidate for vice president of the United States of America. The elections were the first held by the new nation. George Washington was a logical choice for a presidential candidate. He was the only person on the ballot for president and

In 1788, the Founding Fathers of the United States had to decide how a president would be elected. If a president were elected by majority vote, then presidents might often come from states with large populations. So Congress created the Electoral College. Each state would have votes equal to its number of senators (always two) plus its number of representatives (based on population). This made the small states and the large states happy. The Electoral College still exists today, but it has been revised throughout the years. The first plan lasted through the first four presidential elections.

ended up with 100 percent of the votes.

Voting for vice president took place separately in those days. In addition to Adams, John Hancock of Massachusetts and George Clinton of New York were also on the ballot. Adams won the race for vice president. He received 34 of the 69 votes of the Electoral College, a system of representative voting established in the Constitution. Abigail now entered political life with her husband.

John Adams headed to New York City, the capital of the United States at that time. Unfortunately for the Adamses, the president and vice president had to rent their own houses there. That was fine for George Washington, who was quite wealthy, but for John and Abigail Adams, renting and furnishing another house was an expense they could not afford.

John needed to find a house so Abigail could join him in New York. But Congress was trying to decide on how much salary the vice president should receive, and the Adamses didn't know yet what they could afford. Abigail was still fixing up their new home in Braintree, and John was busy with a new government that needed a lot of his time and attention.

But finally, John found a suitable house on Richmond Hill in what is now Greenwich Village in New York City. Soon, the couple moved in to their

The New York City residence of John and Abigail Adams during the vice presidency

new home. It had an expansive view of the Hudson River and a large garden. Abigail arrived with more than 100 boxes filled with clothes, books, linens, silverware, pots and pans, and china. She filled the

house with many of her children and their families—18 people in all.

Abigail's days as the vice president's wife could have easily been filled with social calls, but she had other ideas in mind. She didn't enjoy socializing with the many people who stopped by. She avoided most visits, preferring that guests leave a calling card, showing they had tried to pay her a visit. Then at about 6 o'clock in the evening—a time when most of the women who called were either out or busy—Abigail would stop by their houses and return their social call. Thus, without having to put up with what she considered tiresome women or tedious gossip, she had fulfilled her social obligations.

Of course, she did not avoid everyone. She welcomed visits from the president and his wife. Abigail still admired George Washington very much. To her, he was "polite with dignity ... distant without Haughtyness, grave without austerity, modest, wise, & Good."

Abigail was also greatly impressed with the first lady, Martha Washington. In a letter to her sister Mary, Abigail described Martha after meeting her for the first time:

> *She is plain in her dress, but that plainness is the best of every article. ... Her Hair*

Abigail Adams admired Martha Washington, the first lady of the United States.

is white, her Teeth beautifull, her person rather short. ... Her manners are modest and unassuming, dignified and feminine.

The following year, in 1790, Congress designated

Philadelphia as the temporary capital of the United States. Congress wanted to build a new city to serve as a permanent capital for the nation, but time was needed to plan and construct it. The site was a piece of swampland along the Potomac River in Virginia. It would be called Washington, District of Columbia, named after the first president and Christopher Columbus. It would become the only city in the United States that is not a part of a state.

John and Abigail Adams now had to move again, this time to Philadelphia into a house on Bush Hill. Where that name came from, Abigail could not imagine, for the hill had few shrubs or trees of any kind. The house was smaller than their home in New York City, the painters were still at work, and the house needed repairs. In addition to those problems, the family and the servants became sick right after they moved in.

Things weren't going very well on the political scene, either. The country was barely off the ground, and already politics was dividing old friends. George Washington and John Adams were Federalists, who favored a strong federal government. Thomas Jefferson and James Madison started a new political party, the Democratic Republicans, who opposed a strong central government.

Things weren't going very well with the Adamses' finances, either. During John's first four-year term as

John Adams was the first vice president of the United States and the second president.

vice president, their expenses had been huge, and they were $2,000 in debt, a lot of money for that time. Peacefield, their home in Braintree, was Abigail's only hope of paying off the debt.

While her husband was still serving as vice president, Abigail returned to Peacefield to try to make a profit from the farmland. She lived there for the next five years, and John visited in the summers. By this time, Braintree had been divided into two towns, and the Adamses' property was now in Quincy.

The Adams children were grown and on their own now. John Quincy Adams was the U.S. minister to Holland, and his brother Thomas was there with him, serving as his secretary. Charles Adams lived in New York, where he was trying to set up a legal practice. Nabby Smith also lived in New York City, where she was raising her two sons, William and John. Her other son Thomas had died in 1791.

In 1795, Nabby gave birth to her fourth child, a daughter named Caroline. Abigail was glad to go to

New York City to help Nabby. While she was there, she also visited her son Charles, who had married Nabby's sister-in-law, Sally Smith, that year. Abigail worried about Charles, though. She noticed that he drank too much alcohol, but she had no control over a 25-year-old man. She tried to help him, but Charles wouldn't listen to her.

The following year, the Adamses' lives again changed when George Washington decided he would not run for president again. Although at that time, presidents could serve for more than two four-year terms, Washington believed that holding the office more than eight years would be like becoming king—the very thing he had fought against.

Candidates were chosen for the next presidential race, and John Adams' name was on the 1796 ballot. Running against him was his former close friend and now political enemy, Thomas Jefferson. By a narrow vote, Adams won the election, and Abigail Adams now stepped into the role of first lady of the United States of America. 🐚

8 FIRST LADY

❧❧❧

Abigail Adams wasn't happy about leaving Peacefield. Trading her quiet life again for the social and political whirl was a poor bargain, she felt. She also worried that with her frank, outspoken nature and her dislike for social duties, she would fail as first lady. She was often ill, which she thought would surely interfere with her duties.

In addition, there were many personal expenses that Abigail and John would have to pay. Abigail believed that the presidency would make them poor, and she was right. The president earned a good annual salary, but the president had to rent a house equal to his high position. He was expected to pay for horses and a carriage, furniture, china, and silverware. Costs for formal dinners, ladies' teas, and

A portrait of Abigail Adams and a companion portrait of her husband by Gilbert Stuart were started in 1800 but not finished until 1815.

other social gatherings came out of the their pocket. They also paid for their own servants to clean, cook, garden, and do other household chores. John and Abigail rented the same house that George and Martha Washington lived in during his presidency. But to John's annoyance, the house needed repairs and cleaning, which added to their costs.

On March 4, 1797, John Adams was inaugurated as second president of the United States. Abigail was not there. She would not go to Philadelphia until the farm was in order. She remained at Peacefield, negotiating new contracts with tenant farmers. Money was tight for everyone, and the farmers were demanding more money and more equipment. One farmer insisted on a new pair of oxen, which Abigail bought because she couldn't afford to lose the farmer. Stone walls needed rebuilding, John's aging mother needed a caretaker, and Abigail had to find someone to live in the house and manage the farm in her absence.

When she finally accomplished all her tasks, she went to Philadelphia, where she approached her role as first lady with the same energy and commitment she had shown as a wife, mother, and farmer. She quickly took on her role as the president's supporter, adviser, and friend. She even stood in for him at times, doing presidential duties such as visiting troops and attending community events.

The first lady's days were very full. She got up at 5 A.M. every day and spent the first three hours in her private time. At 8 A.M., she ate breakfast with the family. In her official duties as first lady, she saw visitors between noon and 2 P.M. At 3 P.M., she enjoyed a large dinner and then returned social calls during the rest of the afternoon. John and Abigail received many social invitations from senators, congressmen, and foreign dignitaries. Even though Abigail considered entertaining an invasion

George and Martha Washington and John and Abigail Adams lived in this Philadelphia house during the presidencies.

83

of their privacy and a demanding chore, the couple entertained often.

No matter how busy she was as first lady, Abigail had time for her children. She often visited Nabby and her husband William. Abigail spent summers at Peacefield and convinced Nabby to spend the summers there with her daughter Caroline. Abigail also visited her son Charles in New York City and again was unhappy with what she found. Despite all his success as a lawyer, Charles had turned into a drunkard. Since the situation was not good for his two children, Abigail took his oldest child, Susan, with her to Quincy, where Susan lived for the rest of her childhood. Charles and Sally's younger child, Abbe, went to live with Sally's mother.

In November 1800, the Adamses moved out of the house in Philadelphia and into the new President's House, later called the White House, in the nation's new capital, Washington, D.C. The home was only partly finished, much like the city itself. Progress on the city was slow. Because there weren't enough homes available, most of the people who worked for the government lived

The city of Washington, D.C., was designed by Pierre Charles L'Enfant, a French engineer and a major in the Continental Army during the Revolutionary War. The city's broad avenues, tidy streets, and open spaces became the setting for the White House and the Capitol.

American architect Samuel Blodget Jr. sketched the west end of the President's House in about 1800, as John and Abigail Adams were getting ready to move in as the first residents.

in nearby cities.

The President's House needed plaster, paint, and furniture in most of the rooms. Living there was difficult—not the elegant life people would expect for a president and a first lady. Abigail Adams wrote her sister Mary, "It is [livable] by fires in every part, thirteen of which we are obliged to keep daily, or sleep in wet and damp places."

Servants had to carry water for bathing and washing from Franklin Park, which was five blocks away. The family entered the house by a makeshift set of wooden stairs, since no permanent staircases

Although Abigail Adams lived in France, England, and several U.S. cities, she always considered Braintree (Quincy), Massachusetts her home.

were finished. The East Room, a large parlor for entertaining, became Abigail's drying room, where she hung wet laundry. Her view of the city from the President's House disturbed her greatly. She saw slaves at work each day, as they toiled to finish building the nation's capital. Even though some of her relatives owned slaves, Abigail had never approved of slavery and spoke out against it often:

*Two of our hardy New England Men would
do as much work in a day as the whole 12
[slaves]. But it is true Republicanism that
drive the slaves half fed, and [with little]
clothing ... whilst an owner walks about idle.*

After just one month in the President's House,
John and Abigail received bad news. They learned
their son Charles had died. Heavy drinking led to
serious illness and then death at just 30 years of age.
In addition, the political mood in Washington had
shifted, and John did not win reelection as president.
Instead, the presidency went to Thomas Jefferson.

This was a bitter loss for Adams. His support of
a strong central government had cost him many
friends, and now the election. Just before leaving
office, he used his presidential right to appoint several people to key government positions. He wanted
a strong central government, and putting people in
these positions before the end of his term might help
retain his political views. President-elect Jefferson
voiced his anger over these "midnight appoint-
ments." Former good friends were now extreme
political enemies. ♋

AND BY THE WAY IN THE
NEW CODE OF LAWS
WHICH I SUPPOSE
IT WILL BE NECESSARY
FOR YOU TO MAKE
I DESIRE YOU WOULD
REMEMBER THE LADIES
AND BE MORE GENEROUS
AND FAVORABLE TO THEM
THAN YOUR ANCESTORS.
DO NOT PUT SUCH UNLIMITED
POWER INTO THE HANDS
OF THE HUSBANDS.
REMEMBER ALL MEN WOULD
BE TYRANTS IF THEY COULD.
IF PARTICULAR CARE AND
ATTENTION IS NOT PAID TO THE
LADIES WE ARE DETERMINED
TO FOMENT A REBELLION
AND WILL NOT HOLD OURSELVES
BOUND BY ANY LAWS IN WHICH
WE HAVE NO VOICE
OR REPRESENTATION.

LETTER TO JOHN ADAMS
MARCH 31, 1776

9 *Chapter* ABIGAIL'S LEGACY

❧❀❧

Abigail Adams was delighted to return to private life at Peacefield in March 1801. She had plenty to do and plenty of company to keep her happy. Her granddaughter Susan was still living with them. Nabby's sons William and John attended a nearby Massachusetts boarding school, at their grandmother's insistence and expense. They visited Peacefield during school breaks; Nabby, Caroline, Sally, and Abbe came in the summers.

John Adams, however, was not as happy as his wife. He no longer held a political office, and he had no job. He filled his time at Peacefield writing long papers defending his actions as president and arguing about what his political enemies were saying about him.

A bronze statue of Abigail Adams stands at the Boston Women's Memorial in Boston, Massachusetts.

Thirty-four-year-old John Quincy Adams returned to Boston that year, after serving four years as minister to Prussia. He brought with him his wife, Louisa Catherine Johnson, whom he had met and married in London. John Quincy planned to open a law office in Boston, but instead, he was elected to the U.S. Senate to represent Massachusetts and was headed to Washington, D.C. He had planned to leave his quiet, shy wife at Peacefield. But Louisa didn't understand Abigail's outspoken manner and chose not to live with her mother-in-law.

Life went by peacefully at the Adams home until 1804, when Abigail learned that Thomas Jefferson's daughter Mary had died. Although Jefferson and the Adamses had not spoken to each other for many years, Abigail's deepest sympathy flowed through her pen. She had taken care of Mary when she was just a young girl visiting her father in Europe. Abigail had shopped for her,

John Quincy Adams and his wife, Louisa Catherine Johnson Adams

dressed her, and cared for her. The child's death encouraged Abigail to write to Jefferson:

> *[P]owerfull feelings of my heart ... called upon me to shed the tear of sorrow over the departed remains, of your beloved and deserving daughter.*

It would be nearly eight years before their friendship with Jefferson would be restored. John Adams and Jefferson then began writing to each other, which continued for the rest of their lives until they died on the same day: July 4, 1826, the 50th anniversary of the Declaration of Independence.

In 1805, Abigail's son Thomas returned to Massachusetts with his new wife, Ann Harrod, to live at Peacefield. Thomas' law practice in Philadelphia had not been successful. Unlike John Quincy's wife, Ann got along well with Abigail and enjoyed the Adams household.

The years passed by quietly at Peacefield. Then came 1811, the worst year for Abigail Adams. Her dear sister Mary Cranch became seriously ill with tuberculosis, a lung disease where the lungs slowly weaken until the victim dies. While Mary lay dying, Abigail's daughter-in-law Sally also became so ill that she required constant nursing.

Then John Adams cut his leg so badly that he,

Abigail "Nabby" Adams (1765-1813), daughter of John and Abigail Adams

too, needed care. Shortly after that, Mary's husband Richard suffered a stroke and died within three days. Mary died a day later. Abigail was beside herself with grief, but the worst news was yet to come.

Nabby and Caroline arrived at Peacefield for a visit. Nabby had been diagnosed with breast cancer and needed surgery. An operation in 1811 was not a simple event. The patient endured the operation awake, since there was no anesthetic to put a person to sleep. Most doctors operated in their exam rooms, not in a hospital operating room. Instruments were not sterilized, so the risk of infection was great. Nabby went through a painful ordeal, and her recovery took months. Throughout the autumn of 1811, Abigail and Caroline cared for Nabby.

It seemed that Nabby's operation had successfully removed the cancer. In 1812, she returned to New York and to a normal life. Several months later, however, the cancer returned and spread throughout her body. She traveled to Peacefield, where she planned to die. Nabby died on August 14, 1813. For Abigail, the loss of her beloved daughter was almost too painful to bear. She said, "I have lost, O what have I not lost in ... my only daughter."

The next five years were burdensome for Abigail Adams. Losing a sister, a brother-in-law, and her daughter nearly destroyed what was left of her fighting spirit. Then in October 1818, Abigail became ill with typhoid fever. The doctor's orders were simple—lie in bed without moving, speaking, or being spoken to. John Adams wrote his concerns to his friend Thomas Jefferson, "The dear partner of my life for fifty-four years as a wife … now lies … forbidden to speak or be spoken to."

Within a week, on October 28, 1818, 73-year-old Abigail Adams died. The courageous patriot and former first lady lost her battle with illness. She left behind a legacy of bravery and political influence that helped shape an entire nation.

Abigail Adams was deeply in love with her husband John, whom she called her dearest friend. After her death, her son John Quincy said:

> *She had been fifty-four years the delight of my father's heart, the sweetener of all his toils, the comforter of all his sorrows, the sharer and heightener of all his joys.*

Intelligent and open-minded, Abigail Adams had served as a strong supporter and adviser to her husband while he was planning a new nation and negotiating peace with other countries. She willingly gave up most of her time with him to help establish a new nation. Although she never knew that her son John Quincy Adams would become the sixth president of the United States, she had taught and prepared him at her kitchen table.

For the sake of freedom, Abigail Adams suffered the hardships of the Revolutionary War and made many sacrifices for her country. She served in many roles—from a farmer milking cows to a first lady entertaining presidents and royalty. She spoke out against slavery and supported the cause of women's rights and education. With the power of her pen and a piece of paper, she influenced the Founding Fathers of the United States and made a difference in history. She once wrote to her son John Quincy:

> These are times in which a genius would wish to live. It is not in the still calm of life, or the repose of a pacific station [peaceful state], that great characters are formed.

Loving, bossy, outspoken, intelligent, hardworking, moral, patriotic—this was Abigail Adams. She was one president's wife and another president's

Abigail Adams is honored on a 1985 postage stamp.

mother. She will always be admired as a courageous patriot and one of the important founding mothers of the United States of America. 🔊

ADAMS' LIFE

1744

Born on November 11 in Weymouth, Massachusetts

1764

Marries John Adams on October 25

1765

Daughter Abigail "Nabby" is born

1750

1749

German writer Johann Wolfgang Goethe is born

1762

Catherine the Great becomes empress of Russia and rules for 34 years

WORLD EVENTS

1767

Son John Quincy
is born

1768

Daughter
Susanna is born

1770

Daughter Susanna
dies at 13 months
old; son Charles is
born

1770

1768

British explorer
Captain James
Cook leaves
England for a
three-year
exploration of
the Pacific

1770

Clergyman and
chemist Joseph
Priestly gives rub-
ber its name when
he discovers it rubs
out pencil marks

ADAMS' LIFE

1772

Son Thomas
Boylston is born

1774

John Adams serves
as representative to
the First Continental
Congress

1775

Battles of Lexington
and Concord start
Revolutionary War;
witnesses the Battle
of Bunker Hill

1775

1775

English novelist
Jane Austen
is born

1772

Poland is partitioned for
the first time between
Prussia and Austria

WORLD EVENTS

1776
Declaration of
Independence
is signed

1783
John Adams signs
the Treaty of Paris,
officially ending the
Revolutionary War

1789
John Adams is
elected first vice
president of the
United States

1785

1776
Scottish economist
Adam Smith
publishes *The Wealth
of Nations*, heralding
the beginning of
modern economics

1789
The French
Revolution begins
with the storming
of the Bastille
prison in Paris

ADAMS' LIFE

1796
Becomes the second first lady of the United States

1800
Moves into a partially finished President's House (now called the White House); son Charles dies

1790
Abigail and John move to Philadelphia, temporary capital of the United States

1795

1791
Austrian composer Wolfgang Amadeus Mozart dies

1795
J. F. Blumenbach writes *The Human Species*, thus laying the foundation of anthropology

1799
The Rosetta stone, which was the key to understanding Egyptian hieroglyphics, is found near Rosetta, Egypt

WORLD EVENTS

1801

Retires to
Peacefield in
Quincy,
Massachusetts

1813

Daughter Abigail
"Nabby" dies from
breast cancer

1818

Dies October 28
from typhoid
fever

1815

1805

General anesthesia
is first used in
surgery

1809

Louis Braille of
France, inventor
of a writing
system for the
blind, is born

1814-1815

European states meet in
Vienna, Austria, to
redraw national borders
after the conclusion of
the Napoleonic Wars

DATE OF BIRTH: November 11, 1744

BIRTHPLACE: Weymouth, Massachusetts

FATHER: Rev. William Smith (1706-1783)

MOTHER: Elizabeth Quincy Smith (1721-1775)

EDUCATION: No formal education

SPOUSE: John Adams (1735-1826)

DATE OF MARRIAGE: October 25, 1764

CHILDREN: Abigail "Nabby" (1765-1813)
John Quincy (1767-1848)
Susanna (1768-1770)
Charles (1770-1800)
Thomas Boylston (1772-1832)

DATE OF DEATH: October 28, 1818

PLACE OF BURIAL: Quincy, Massachusetts

In the Library

Bober, Natalie S. *Abigail Adams: Witness to a Revolution*. New York: Simon & Schuster Children's, 1998.

Davis, Kate. *Abigail Adams*. San Diego: Blackbirch Press, 2002.

Ferris, Jeri Chase. *Remember the Ladies: A Story About Abigail Adams*. Minneapolis: Carolrhoda Books, 2000.

Santella, Andrew. *John Adams*. Minneapolis: Compass Point Books, 2003.

St. George, Judith. *John and Abigail Adams: An American Love Story*. New York: Holiday House, 2001.

Look for more Signature Lives
books about this era:

Alexander Hamilton: *Founding Father and Statesman*

Benedict Arnold: *From Patriot to Traitor*

Benjamin Franklin: *Scientist and Statesman*

Ethan Allen: *Green Mountain Rebel*

John Hancock: *Signer for Independence*

John Paul Jones: *Father of the American Navy*

Martha Washington: *First Lady of the United States*

Mercy Otis Warren: *Author and Historian*

Phillis Wheatley: *Slave and Poet*

Samuel Adams: *Patriot and Statesman*

Thomas Paine: *Great Writer of the Revolution*

On the Web

For more information on *Abigail Adams*, use FactHound to track down Web sites related to this book.

1. Go to *www.facthound.com*
2. Type in a search word related to this book or this book ID: 0756509815
3. Click on the *Fetch It* button.

FactHound will find the best Web sites for you.

Historic Sites

Adams National Historical Park
135 Adams St.
Quincy, MA 02169
617/770-1175
To view the home of four generations of the Adams family

The Abigail Adams Birthplace
180 Norton St.
Weymouth, MA 02188
781/335-4205
To view the Smith home where Abigail Smith Adams was born

anesthetic
a substance that reduces sensitivity to pain, sometimes with loss of consciousness

arsenal
a storehouse of weapons and ammunition

brand
to mark the skin with a hot iron, sometimes as a mark of disgrace

cobbler
someone who makes or repairs footwear

courtship
the process of seeking to win a promise of marriage

diplomacy
skill in handling affairs without causing hostility or conflict (often between nations)

dysentery
a disease of the intestines caused by infection

militia
a military force made up of volunteers

minutemen
a group of men ready to take up arms at a minute's notice during the American Revolution

representation
the right of being represented by someone, especially in the legislature of a government

typhoid fever
a serious and sometimes fatal bacterial infection of the digestive system caused by contaminated food or water

Chapter 1

Page 12, line 10: "Letter from Abigail Adams to John Adams, 18-20 June 1775." *Adams Family Papers*, www.masshist.org/digital-adams/aea/cfm/doc.cfm?id=L17750618aa

Page 15, line 3: Cokie Roberts. *Founding Mothers*. New York: HarperCollins Publishers Inc., 2004, p. xvi.

Page 15, line 11: *Founding Mothers*, p. 61.

Page 15, line 14: Ibid.

Page 15, line 19: Ibid., p. 76.

Page 15, line 23: Ibid.

Chapter 2

Page 26, line 4: L. H. Butterfield & Marc Friedlaender, eds. *The Book of Abigail and John*. Cambridge, Mass.: Harvard University Press, 1975, p. 17.

Page 26, line 8: Ibid., pp. 18-19.

Page 27, line 8: Ibid.

Chapter 3

Page 34, line 7: Lynne Withey. *Dearest Friend: A Life of Abigail Adams*. New York: Touchstone, 2001, p. 22.

Page 34, line 22: Edith B. Gelles. *Portia: The World of Abigail Adams*. Bloomington: Indiana University Press, 1992, p. 28.

Page 36, line 12: Ibid., p. 28.

Chapter 4

Page 43, line 1: *The Book of Abigail and John*, p. 47.

Page 43, line 14: Ibid., p. 53.

Page 44, line 21: Ibid., pp. 53-54.

Page 45, line 9: Frank Shuffelton, ed. *The Letters of John and Abigail Adams*. New York: Penguin Books, 2004, p. 3.

Page 46, line 10: Ibid., pp. 38-39.

Page 47, line 6: Ibid., pp. 44-46.

Chapter 5

Page 50, line 11: *The Book of Abigail and John*, p. 84.

Page 51, line 6: Ibid., p. 85.

Page 52, line 2: *The Letters of John and Abigail Adams*, p. 63.

Page 52, line 13: Ibid., p. 77.

Page 53, line 7: Ibid., pp. 72-73.

Page 54, line 15: Ibid., p. 93.

Page 55, line 5: Ibid., p. 137.

Page 58, line 2: *The Book of Abigail and John*, p. 121.

Page 59, line 2: Ibid., p. 57.

Page 59, line 5: *Founding Mothers*, p. 75.

Chapter 6

Page 64, line 2: David McCullough. *John Adams*. New York: Touchstone, 2001, p. 203.

Page 69, line14: *Dearest Friend: A Life of Abigail Adams*, p. 201.

Chapter 7

Page 75, line 19: Phyllis Lee Levin. *Abigail Adams: A Biography*. New York: St. Martin's Press, 1987, p. 264.

Page 75, line 26: Ibid., p. 259.

Chapter 8

Page 85, line 6: *John Adams*, p. 553.

Page 87, line 1: Ibid., p. 553.

Chapter 9

Page 91, line 3: Lester J. Cappon, ed. *The Adams-Jefferson Letters: The Complete Correspondence Between Thomas Jefferson and Abigail and John Adams*. Chapel Hill, NC: University of North Carolina Press, 1988, p. 269.

Page 93, line 4: *Portia: The World of Abigail Adams*, p. 162.

Page 93, line 13: Ibid., p. 168.

Page 93, line 24: *John Adams*, p. 622.

Page 94, line 20: *The Book of Abigail and John*, p. 253.

Select Bibliography

Cappon, Lester J., ed. *The Adams-Jefferson Letters: The Complete Correspondence Between Thomas Jefferson and Abigail and John Adams.* Chapel Hill, N.C.: University of North Carolina Press, 1988.

Butterfield, L. H., Marc Friedlaender, and Mary-Jo Kline, eds. *The Book of Abigail and John: Selected Letters of the Adams Family 1762-1784.* Cambridge, Mass.: Harvard University Press, 1975.

Gelles, Edith B. *Portia: The World of Abigail Adams.* Bloomington, Ind.: University of Indiana Press, 1992.

Levin, Phyllis Lee. *Abigail Adams: A Biography.* New York: St. Martin's Press, 1987.

McCullough, David. *John Adams.* New York: Touchstone, 2001.

Shuffelton, Frank, ed. *The Letters of John and Abigail Adams.* New York: Penguin Books, 2004.

Withey, Lynne. *Dearest Friend: A Life of Abigail Adams.* New York: Touchstone, 2001.

Barbara A. Somervill has been writing for more than 30 years. She has written newspaper and magazine articles, video scripts, and books for children. She enjoys writing about science and investigating people's lives for biographies. She lives with her husband in South Carolina.

Image Credits